The CLOSENESS *of* GOD

The Art and Inspiration of Sieger Köder

The CLOSENESS *of* GOD

The Art and Inspiration of Sieger Köder

Gemma Simmonds

BOOKS & MEDIA

This edition published in the United Kingdom in 2013
Pauline Books & Media
Slough SL3 6BS

Graphic design Mary Louise Winters fsp

Scripture texts from the Christian Community Bible

ISBN 9781904785675

BOOKS & MEDIA
Middle Green, Slough SL3 6BS – UK
0044 (0) 1753 577629
www.pauline-uk.org
email: marketing@pauline-uk.org

Pauline Books & Media is an expression of the ministry of the Daughters of St Paul, a group of religious sisters whose ministry is to proclaim the Good News of Jesus Christ using the most effective means of communication.

The CLOSENESS *of* GOD

the promise

A Journey of Faith and a Dream Fulfilled

At various times in the past and in various different ways,
God spoke to our ancestors through the prophets:
but in our own time... he has spoken to us through his Son.

Hebrews 1:1–2

Seeing is believing, says popular wisdom. In a world full of words, Sieger Köder's paintings invite us to approach Scripture with our eyes. The directness of his painting helps us to open our hearts to ancient stories and make them our own. These images, from the promise made to Abraham to its fulfilment in Mary's Son, draw us near to the mystery of the Word of God made human flesh for our sake.

In the Scriptures we witness the struggle to believe, to hope, to follow, and we hear echoes of our own struggles. We meditate with our eyes and find new aspects of truth revealed in our search for faith. The message underlying the story of each image is that God is with us. In all times and seasons of the year we can reflect on how God's dream for creation was worked out in particular times and places and people. We can find resonances in these stories of what is at work in our own world and time. God's invitation to us is to look for the story beneath the story, the picture behind the picture. It is our own story, as we, too, are called to leave what is safe and familiar to journey with God.

As we meditate with the help of this booklet, may we find our courage strengthened and our hopes fulfilled.

I know the plans
I have in mind
for you –
it is the LORD
who speaks –
plans for peace,
not disaster,
reserving a future
full of hope
for you.

Jeremiah 29:11

covenant

My hands are empty
as I stand before you, O God.
My past is behind me,
gone beyond recall.
My present unsure,
my future unknown.
How can I be certain
that my life has been worthwhile?
How can I find you
and be sure of your will?

Within this emptiness you promise
a life fruitful as the countless stars.

All you ask is that I trust your promise,
that I take the risk of believing.

'Leave all that is safe and familiar,
dare to walk into the unknown...'
Where can I find such faith,
hope and courage?

You call me by name.
You offer a new homeland
for my heart.
My faith can even strengthen others.
You open to me a future
full of blessing and hope.

With my open hands
and open heart
I feel vulnerable before you.
But the stars in the sky
are a sign
of your faithfulness.

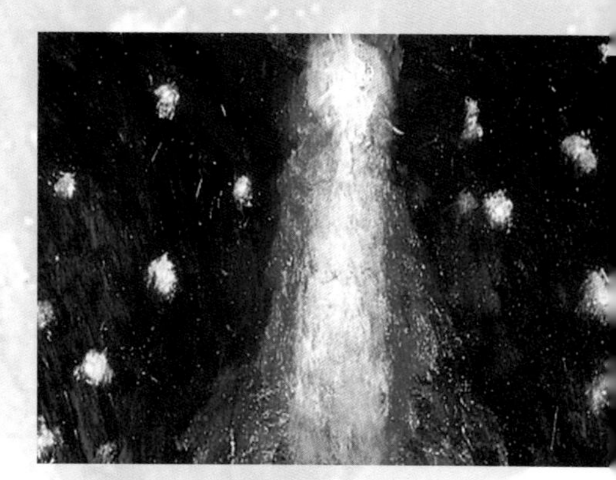

covenant

The story of Abraham and Sarah reveals a pattern often repeated in Scripture and in our own lives. God is not dismayed by our fear, our clutching after false securities, our lack of faith and courage. We are called to travel without maps, to make the path by walking. We are offered no certainty but promised a future where our hopes will be transformed and fulfilled. Abraham and Sarah's descendants see the promise unfold, despite lives complicated by misfortune, weakness and life's stumbling blocks. They struggle with the mystery of human suffering, but God's promise is fulfilled for each of us in the person of Jesus. His life, death and resurrection are the guarantee of an everlasting covenant of love, sealed in his blood.

Scripture...

God's promise

May God give you peace – he who brought back from among the dead Jesus our Lord,
the great Shepherd of the sheep, whose blood seals the eternal covenant.
He will train you in every good work, that you may do his will,
for it is he who works in us what pleases him, through Jesus Christ,
to whom all glory be for ever and ever. Amen.

Hebrews 13:20–21

We pray...

Pilgrim God,
you travel with us
into an unknown future,
strengthening us
by your love.

Be our strong companion,
a light in our darkness.

In your Son Jesus
may we find the new
and everlasting promise
of your love.

Truly
the Lord
is in this place
and
I never knew it!

Genesis 28:16

vision

A lonely traveller lies down to rest,
dreaming of a ladder
between heaven and earth.

Hands reach upward in entreaty,
downward in compassion.
Blessed are those
who know their need of God!

Do we recognise the pattern
of God's presence in our lives?
Can we look back and say:
'God was there'?
We cry: 'Where are you, God?
Where were you when I needed you?'
God whispers in response:
'I am here beside you –
open your eyes, open your heart.'

Looking back on the events
and encounters of each day
we recognise God's presence.

Lived experience
brings God's word to life.
God's word sheds light
on our lived experience.
Hands going upward
and downward
between heaven and earth
— our search for meaning
and God's answer
in loving presence,
in good times and in bad.

vision

Jacob is every human being trying to make sense of life. We look back on events in search of their meaning. But our own fixed interpretation can blind us to God's unfolding purpose.

As with the disciples at Emmaus, One walks alongside us unrecognised, opening the Scriptures to us and revealing God's unseen presence at work in our lives. Our lives are Scriptures in themselves, with their joyful, sorrowful and glorious mysteries. Without denying hard truths or tidying up the script, we can nevertheless learn to say: 'Truly God was here, and I didn't know it!'

Scripture...

Journey of faith

O Lord, you know me: you have scrutinised me.
You know when I sit and when I rise: beforehand you discern my thoughts.
You observe my activities and time of rest; you are familiar with all my ways...
Your knowledge leaves me astounded; it is too high for me to reach.
Where else could I go from your Spirit?
Where could I flee from your presence?

Psalm 139:1–7

We pray...

God of our hopes

and dreams,

we search for meaning

and long to know

that you are present

in our lives.

By the power of your Spirit

make us dreamers

of your dream for ourselves

and for our world.

Give us the faith and vision

to make that dream

a reality.

In meadows
of green grass
he lets me lie.
To the waters
of repose
he leads me;
there he revives
my soul.

Psalm 23:2–3

green pastures

A desert people sings
of God leading them
to green pastures by living streams.

A hungry world longs to be nourished.
Those who hunger and thirst for justice
long for the kingdom.
The poor, guests at God's banquet,
with tears of suffering wiped away.

From Christ's wounds
living waters flow.
Our loaves and fishes seem
so inadequate for the task.
Can we believe that there will be
basketfuls left over?

God has no hands but ours
to transform the world,
no voice but ours
to sing God's song in an alien land.
In the frantic rhythm of our world God
leads us to still waters.

In the valley of darkness
our shepherd is near,
staff at the ready...
God fills the starving
with good things,
sends the rich away empty.

Do we know what is
starving within us,
what is sick with overfeeding?
What needs to be filled,
what needs to be emptied
so that God's Spirit
can pour through us like water?

green pastures

Psalm 23 proclaims the hope for which we long – that God will be our everlasting rest and dwelling-place. God promises us an eternal home in a heart that has always got room to spare: but this is not just so that we can lie back in comfort and complacency. We are given living water to be refreshment for others. We are given a dwelling place in God so that we can be home for others. The Eucharist gives us power to become bread for the world, good shepherds in our own turn.

Scripture...

God's dwelling place

Let mutual love continue. Do not neglect to offer hospitality;
you know some people have entertained angels without knowing it.
Remember prisoners as if you were with them in chains,
and the same for those who are suffering.
Remember that you also have a body.
Do not depend on money.
Be content with having enough for today for God has said:
'I will never forsake you or abandon you,' and we shall confidently answer:
'The Lord is my helper, I will not fear.'

Hebrews 13:1–3;5–6

We pray...

Help us, O God,

to let go of noise

and hurry and sink into

your quiet rest.

In our valleys of darkness

lead us to living streams.

Help us to hunger

and thirst for you,

knowing you as

Gift and Giver.

Anoint us and choose us

to be bread for our world.

Help us to find

our home in you.

Miriam led them in the refrain: 'Sing of the LORD: he has covered himself in glory, horse and rider he has thrown into the sea.'

Exodus 15:20–21

jubilation

Have you ever wanted
to sing for joy or dance in the streets?
At football matches each goal
is greeted with song and celebration.

Do we ever sing and dance
for sheer delight
before the Lord of the Dance?
God delights in us,
dancing as on a day of festival.
Can we do the same,
or is our God too solemn for that?

Do we know what true joy is?

It is easy to cry out for God
in our need, forgetting to give thanks
in times of blessing.

The more I acknowledge God's gifts,
the more I learn to love the Giver.

God has no need of our gratitude,
but thanksgiving
opens our hearts to joy.

Creation reveals a playful God,
delighting in wondrous variety,
whose wisdom is at play
in all that is made.

That includes us.

jubilation

True joy is not a matter of false exhilaration. We can be in deep distress and still be aware of God's presence. In the red dawn behind Miriam we see the Egyptian pyramids, symbol of slavery. The God of freedom invites us to detect providence in our lives. We fear to sound smug if we proclaim the goodness of God. Perhaps we don't want to tempt providence and rejoice, in case bad times come. But we are not called to be prophets of doom and gloom.

If Jesus really is the joy of our desiring, then our greatest gift to the world will be to share our joy as we place our hope in God, the light shining in the darkness. Jesus does not promise a life without difficulty, but to those willing to take up the cross daily, he promises Easter joy, a joy that will be complete.

Scripture...

God of joy

To you, O Lord, I called; to you I begged for mercy;
hear, O Lord, and have mercy on me; O Lord, be my protector.
But now, you have turned my mourning into rejoicing;
you have taken off my sackcloth and wrapped me in the garments of gladness.
And so my soul, no longer silent, now sings praise without ceasing.
O Lord, my God, forever will I give you thanks.

Psalm 30:8,10–12

We pray...

God of joy and gladness,

you promise to turn

our mourning

into rejoicing,

our tears into

songs of thanksgiving.

Teach us to be thoughtful

without being morose

and cheerful

without being false.

May we thank you daily

for the gift of life itself

and all that life brings.

Blessed is she
who believed
that the promise
made her
by the Lord
would be fulfilled.

Luke 1:45

magnificat

Two women meet,
clinging to one another
in their need of reassurance,
bodies speaking loudly as words.

Childless women feel the leap of life within.
Hope springs to life in the power of the Spirit,
an incredible promise now fulfilled.

Years later, their sons meet.
One 'like us in all things but sin' joins
repentant crowds, asking for baptism.

The prophet cries out in amazement
and shame –
the Lord of creation submits
to human judgment.

God's presence on earth
turns the world's priorities upside down.
The powerful are brought low,
the poor exalted.

The first will be last
and the last first.
The Son of God is baptised,
the Creator becomes a carpenter.
Rejoice, most highly favoured,
the Lord is with you,
Emmanuel – God is with us.

magnificat

Mary's magnificat proclaims the reversal of values in a world where the strongest survive and the poor are trampled upon. An insignificant woman exults in the power of God, shining through her human weakness. Jesus declares his solidarity with humanity, each one of us, through him, a beloved daughter or son in whom God is well pleased. Each human encounter can become an Annunciation, a Visitation. 'The God in me greets the God in you', goes the Eastern greeting. How often do we meet another, and honour God in that person? If we really believed and acted on this, our world would be transformed.

Scripture...

God's promise fulfilled

Mary then set out for a town in the hills of Judah.
She entered the house of Zechariah and greeted Elizabeth.
When Elizabeth heard Mary's greeting, the baby leapt in her womb.
Elizabeth was filled with the Holy Spirit and giving a loud cry, said,
'You are most blessed among women and blessed is the fruit of your womb!
Blessed are you who believed that the Lord's word would come true!'

Luke 1:39–45

We pray...

God of greeting,

you are at the heart

of each human encounter.

Help us to recognise

your human face,

seeing in others' features

and our own

your image and likeness.

Like Mary, may we believe

that the promise

you make to us

will be fulfilled.

For there is
a child
born for us,
a son
is given to us.

Isaiah 9:6

God with us

At the dead of night,
in the darkness and cold a child is born.
The promise at last becomes
flesh and blood, spirit and truth.

Joseph sleeps,
his dreams bringing wisdom.
Mary treasures her baby,
pondering in her heart
the meaning of God's gift.
A happy Christmas scene –
a comforting fairy tale for children,
but above mother and child
loom the cross-beams of the stable.
The crib and the cross bear his name:
Jesus of Nazareth, King of the Jews.

His birth for her the beginning
of a lifelong journey,
the truth only learned on Calvary,
'Behold your Son.'

Here is one like us in all things,
like us, born to die.

Are we witnessing a birth or a death?
What is born
when Jesus comes into our world?
What has to die?
This mystery of birth and death
is a promise and a challenge.
A sign of contradiction
piercing our hearts with a sword.
Inviting us to make the journey
with Mary and Joseph...

God with us

Our nativity scene can often seem like a children's story, a magic tale where we all live happily ever after. Instead for Mary and Joseph it was the beginning of a lifelong pilgrimage: Egypt, Nazareth, Jerusalem, Cana, Golgotha. Mary's questions, begun at the Annunciation, only get deeper, 'How can this be...?' Where she goes, we follow – from manger to tomb and beyond. Trusting in God's promise, even without fully understanding, she shows us the path of true discipleship. By living our human life to the full, Jesus transforms death into life, human weakness into divine strength. The crib and the cross are one.

Scripture...

Light in our darkness

Yes, God so loved the world that he gave his only Son that whoever believes in him may not be lost, but may have eternal life. God did not send the Son into the world to condemn the world; instead through him the world is to be saved. Whoever believes in him will not be condemned.

John 3:16–18

We pray...

Christ our Morning Star –

to you

our deepest night

is as clear as day.

We adore you, O Christ,

and we praise you,

because by your life

and your death,

you have redeemed

the world.

the invitation

A Call to Life

Oh, come to the water all you who are thirsty;

though you have no money, come!

Pay attention, come to me;

listen, and your soul will live.

Isaiah 55:1–3

In St Augustine's writings God says, 'You would not be seeking me if I had not already found you.' The Bible is a book of hide and seek, where God seeks us and we run away, and we so often seek the divine in what is less than God. We constantly try to cut God down to our own size, but God surprises us with ways that are not ours. Sieger Köder paints a series of encounters or parables where this interplay of loss and meeting is explored. There is loneliness and intimacy, solitude and reconciliation, compassion and rejection. He paints around the theme of masks, reflections, the Harlequin – the dreamer in the coat of many colours who lies beneath our many disguises. Within these paintings lies an invitation. It is God's initiative in a relationship of truth and love.

The Old Testament begins with God and humankind walking in quiet friendship in the cool of the evening. Nakedness is nothing to be feared, intimacy is easy. Later we are shown God 'again and again offering a covenant' in the hope of renewing the bond that was lost. We are urged to seek God, and shown with what persistence God seeks us. The New Testament shows us encounters between Jesus and people whose lives are transformed through meeting Him. God calls us to strip away the masks, dare to go into a place of depth, of solitude and intimacy, and discover our truest self in relationship with our Creator. God calls us out of false images of self into the sometimes painful journey towards the truth which sets us free. It is never too late, the distance is never too large to be bridged. As we meditate with the help of these pictures, may we have our ears and eyes opened to the invitation of God.

It was you
who created
my inmost self,
knit me together
in my mother's womb.

Psalm 139:13

insight

Staring into the depths,
what do we see?

The journey inward
is the hardest of all;
walls of self-protection,
built over the years,
block out light and truth.
Loneliness aches,
emptiness rings hollow,
but ours is not the only face
reflected in the living water.
We are never entirely alone.

A voice breaks through the silence:
'I'm thirsty –
will you give me a drink?'

What do I have that God could want?
A heart ready to receive,
open to possibilities.

'If you only knew the gift of God,
and who it is
that is speaking to you...'

Can we recognise
the one whose invitation
echoes in our hearts?

Can we share
the gift once received?

insight

The Samaritan woman knows shame and loneliness, the pain of rejection and abandonment. Going to the well at midday she is sure to see no one, keeping herself to herself. An unexpected invitation is given: to listen and be heard, to offer the simple gift of water to a thirsty stranger, to share her longing for truth, her search for answers, to move from the limits of a worship restricted by custom to knowing God in spirit and in truth, to allow the living Spirit of God to well up from within. Her response becomes a gift for others, an invitation freely passed on, 'Come and see...' Our hearts are made for God, and only God's Spirit can conquer our restlessness.

Scripture...

Gift of discernment

We are weak, but the Spirit comes to help us.
How to ask? And what shall we ask for?
We do not know, but the Spirit intercedes for us without words, as if with groans. And he who sees inner secrets knows the desires of the Spirit,
for he asks for the holy ones what is pleasing to God.

Romans 8:26–27

We pray...

God of the deep places,

we long to worship you

in spirit and truth.

Help us to honour

our own questions

and those of others.

Teach us to know you

as Giver and Gift.

Look,
I am standing
at the door,
knocking.
If one of you
hears me calling
and opens the door
I will come in
to share a meal.

Revelation 3:20

turning point

Eyes agog,
fingers pointing,
ears stretched to hear the scandal.

'Have you seen?
Did you hear?
Well, I never, how disgraceful!'

A splinter in another's eye
is easier to see
than a plank of wood in our own.

Leafy sycamores and dense crowds
are no hiding places
from God's invitation.

'I want to be your guest today –
will you let me in?'
What a shocking thing,
to play host to God!
Who could be worthy?

Condemnation
by the self-righteous
pains God
more than the shame of the sinful.

'Behold, I stand at the door
and knock...'
Who are the real outsiders?

turning point

Most of us have so many inner voices of condemnation – we don't need them from outside. Yet judging and condemning others can also be an irresistible pastime, an effective distraction from our own shortcomings. Great saints believe that they are great sinners. This is no false modesty. The closer we get to God the more we are overwhelmed by God's utter otherness, God's holiness and our weakness. A deep sense of sin can be a wonderful gift when it leads us to realise that we are loved, understood and forgiven sinners. It liberates us from our attempts at self-redemption, doomed as they are to failure. It leads to joyful gratitude in the face of undeserved and unconditional love. Its fruits are joy and true humility.

Scripture...

Open the door, put on the new self

Clothe yourselves, then, as is fitting for God's chosen people, holy, and beloved of him.
Put on compassion, kindness, humility, meekness and patience.
As the Lord has forgiven you, forgive one another.
When you have put on all these, take love as your belt
so that the dress be perfect.
May the peace of Christ overflow in your hearts;
for this end you were called to be one body. And be thankful.

Colossians 3:12–15

We pray...

God of the moments

when we feel so small,

you are

our 'homeliest home'.

Give us the courage

to open the door

of our hearts

when you knock,

pleading to be our guest.

Anyone who says
'I love God'
and hates his brother,
is a liar,
since no one
who fails
to love the brother
whom he can see
can love God
whom he has not seen.

I John 4:20

home

Insiders and outsiders,
belonging and feeling left out.
Where do we feel at home?
Where do we feel lost?

A sinner forgiven,
a lost one embraced,
cause for rejoicing,
or cause for resentment?

God's sun shines on good
and bad alike,
God's rain falls on the honest
and dishonest.
The same pay for a day's work
or an hour's –
it's not fair!

God is not fair
by our standards,
not vengeful or generous
by our measure.

What about all the hard work, the sacrifice?
What is the point of trying to be good?

'What I want is mercy, not sacrifice.
Be compassionate,
as your Father is compassionate.'

God does not spurn a contrite spirit
and a humble heart.

home

Family life can challenge and distress, as well as bring joy. Old wounds and resentments surface, familiar faces mirror our own, showing us our shortcomings, real or imagined. It requires generosity to rejoice for another's good fortune. We need faith and imagination to believe that 'the family problem' can be healed. Maybe we need healing too. Being 'the good one' or 'the black sheep' of a family are both problematic. God is greater than our notions of virtue or vice. God's grace invites us to drop the roles and masks and become our truest self. This liberates us to let others be as God sees them.

Scripture...

God's household

And now I kneel in the presence of the Father
from whom every family in heaven and on earth has received its name.
May he strengthen in you the inner self through his Spirit, according to the riches of his glory;
may Christ dwell in your hearts through faith; may you be rooted and founded in love.
All of this so that you may understand with all the holy ones
the width, the length, the height and the depth –
in a word, that you may know the love of Christ which surpasses all knowledge,
that you may be filled and reach the fullness of God.

Ephesians 3:14–19

We pray...

God of compassion,

your merciful eyes

see not what we are,

nor what we have been,

but what we long to be –

loving and beloved,

forgiven and accepted.

Give us a mind and heart

as free as your own,

open

to the possibility of change.

There is more rejoicing in heaven
over one sinner who repents
than over ninety-nine upright people
who have no need of repentance.

Luke 15:7

celebrate

How dreadful it is to lose something.
Treasured possessions,
only of sentimental value,
but so precious.
A beloved face,
no longer there,
an empty place at the family table,
a job, a home, a native land, an identity.

Loss goes deep –
a part of ourselves goes missing.

God grieves for us like this,
counts the search worthwhile,
even just for one,
every individual unique and precious.

God never loses hope,
even when others give up.

'Just one more chance,
one more try,'
and another...
and another...

To God there is no one like me.

Our hidden self,
our lost innocence,
treasures torn from us
by life's mischances,
all rediscovered in the seeker God
when we let ourselves be found.

The sense of loss is one of life's greatest pains. We mourn deeply in the face of bereavements: redundancy, the break-up of relationships, the loss of home or health leaves us numb and empty. The Gospel parables emphasise the worth to God of our uniqueness: one coin, one sheep, one sinner. God longs for each one of us to turn and be saved. Faith does not protect us from loss or the consequences of sinfulness. God does not want us to despair or punish ourselves for our mistakes and misfortunes, but rejoices when we come home, finding in him a safe anchorhold for our lives.

Scripture...

Rejoice!

Rejoice always; pray without ceasing and give thanks to God at every moment. This is the will of God, your vocation as Christians.

1 Thessalonians 5:16–18

Rejoice in the Lord always. I say it again: rejoice!
May everyone experience your gentle and understanding heart.
The Lord is near: do not be anxious about anything.
In everything resort to prayer and supplication
together with thanksgiving and bring your requests before God.

Philippians 4:4–6

We pray...

Shepherd God,

we stray

on many paths

and grieve

for all our losses.

You consider

each one of us

worth saving.

Come to find us,

call us home to you,

who rejoice

at our return.

The heart knows
its own grief best,
nor can a stranger
share its joy...
even in laughter
the heart
finds sadness.

Proverbs 14:10;13

real me

Contrasting colours,
contrasting masks.
Celebration and mourning,
truth and semblance.

Few experiences are
wholly sad or joyful.
Life can be a fearful affair.
Put on the make-up,
put on the war-paint
put on the mask and hide!

Personalities worn like coats,
hiding behind a title, a role,
safe beyond criticism and self-doubt.

A quiet invitation pierces our defences:
'Be still,
draw near,
let me tell you who you really are.'

There is one place
where it is safe to remove the mask,
one gaze we need not fear to meet,
only one who calls us
by our true name...

real me

Children growing to adulthood through adolescence try on different personalities, changing in response to a mood or a particular environment. Older people can do that too, through insecurity or fear of being judged. A social mask can feel protective, a defence in times of vulnerability. Playing a role can become easier than risking being true to ourselves.
God created Adam and Eve naked. God's loving gaze invites us to be our authentic selves without fear of rejection or judgment. If we can learn to see ourselves with God's loving and compassionate eyes, we may find the freedom and confidence not to have to pretend for others.

Scripture...

Taking off my mask

By the grace of God you have been saved through faith.
This has not come from you: it is God's gift.
This was not the result of your work, so you are not to feel proud.
What we are is God's work.
He has created us in Christ Jesus for the good works he has prepared
that we should devote ourselves to them.

Ephesians 2:8–10

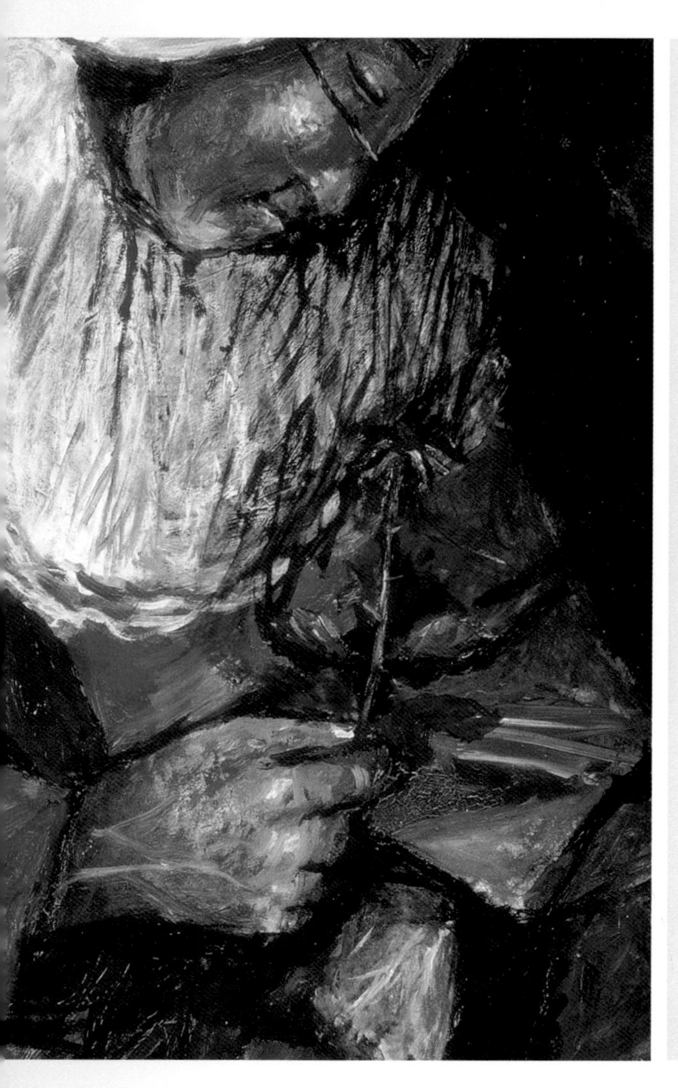

We pray...

God of truth,

unmask

our false identities,

our false securities.

Hide us

in the shadow

of your wings.

Give us the courage

to be real.

When you pray,
go to your
private room,
shut yourself in,
and so
pray to your Father
who is
in that secret place.

Matthew 6:6

hidden place

We wear many disguises:
suits for work,
uniforms of power,
habits and collars,
labels and badges,
roles and titles,
coats of many colours.

Is there a dreamer inside?
Is there a dwelling-place
in our hearts
where the God
who works in secret
can enter?
Do we dare to be naked
in our own inner room?

An invitation is offered
to go into that secret place:
off come the painful shoes,
the heavy clothes,
the tight hat.

A naked child again –
free to be me,
free to give expression
to all that is most precious.

Our hidden self grows strong,
planted and built on love,
rooted in God,
beyond all disguising.

hidden place

Jesus' teaching on prayer is extraordinarily simple and intimate. He has no time for pious pretences, long-winded devotions or extravagant gestures. For him prayer is a place hidden in the human heart, where we can take off our protective covering and open ourselves to receive God's mercy and love. Simple words of love and need: for forgiveness, for daily bread, for the finding of God's will. Simple gestures of thanksgiving and praise, desire and generosity, without the need to impress or force another's gratitude. This is where God seeks us and hopes to be found.

Scripture...

Our Father

When you pray, do not use a lot of words, as the pagans do,
for they hold that the more they say, the more chance they have of being heard. Do not be like them. Your Father knows what you need, even before you ask him.

This, then, is how you should pray:
Our Father in heaven, holy be your name,
your kingdom come and your will be done, on earth as in heaven.
Give us today our daily bread.
Forgive us our debts just as we have forgiven those who are in debt to us.
Do not bring us to the test but deliver us from the evil one.

Matthew 6:7–13

We pray...

Lover of our souls

and intimate friend,

give strength

to our hidden self.

Plant us

and build us

in love

so that we

can come to fullness

in you.

the closeness of God

A Moment of Encounter

My heart has said of you,
'Seek his face.'
LORD, I do seek your face;
do not hide your face from me.

Psalm 27:8–9

Since the beginning of human society, we have turned to painting to express what is deepest within us. In every age and within every system of belief, human beings have reached out in search of the Other. This quest for encounter with God is something more than the primitive desire of cave-dwellers for some warmth and light to keep the shadows at bay. It has occupied the greatest minds and hearts of human history. It is driven by a need for meaning, a thirst for understanding and a longing for intimacy. Our human condition compels us to search for answers to our sense of isolation and the experience of suffering. Our hopes and dreams however also draw us to God, as does our capacity to aspire to something greater than the here and now.

This section illustrates moments of encounter with God as found in various Bible stories. Each encounter is different, portraying the whole spectrum of human responses to this terrifying and fascinating mystery. It is not only Elijah or Peter or the disciples who meet God but every man and every woman. In the midst of life's storms, in the darkness of failure or the intimacy of a meal with friends, our untamable, unexpected God is there. There is no aspect of human life and emotion where God is not present. Yet God's way of being present often confounds our expectations and our preconceived notions. Moments of joy, of intimacy, of confusion and despair can be the opportunity for a deeper awareness of God's presence.

In a mixture of Old and New Testament scenes the theme of the unexpected God is explored. While they fit well into the themes of the Lenten liturgical cycle, the themes and Scripture references can be used throughout the year, for personal and group reflection of any kind. The paintings reveal something new each time we contemplate them, since we ourselves are a different person each time we look. Our senses are a window that opens onto God. As we allow the passion and strength of Sieger Köder's paintings to speak to us, the word of God, alive and active as it is, comes to life in new ways and draws us close to the God who is always waiting.

My eyes
have grown dim
with looking up.
Lord,
I am overwhelmed,
come to my help.

Isaiah 38:14

trusting

Out of the depths a cry –
'Lord, hear my voice!'
Other voices
drown out the voice of hope.
Dark figures and faces of mockery.
Where do they come from?
Outside or deep within?

Voices speaking in unison:
'You're no good,
you'll never change,
we'll watch you fail...'

Fearful hands,
clenched with insecurity –
'I must protect myself,
hide my real face,
disguise my shame.'

If God takes note of our sins,
which of us
could survive such scrutiny?

God's justice
challenges us with the truth,
yet God's mercy is as sure as the dawn.

Light falls on the upturned face:
'Look up! Do not be afraid! I am here.
As far as East is from West,
so far do I remove your sins.'

trusting

Many of us carry around critical voices playing within our heads – discouragement, harsh self-judgment sapping our confidence and hope. How can we face the truth without despair? How can we live with the consequences of our sinfulness? Some of us have been taught to fear God as an all-seeing, stern judge. For others, sin is not important – God is love, after all... Neither extreme leads anywhere helpful. But the gift of courage and honesty, facing our sinfulness in the light of God's mercy, is the beginning of a powerful grace of gratitude and trust. God knows our weakness and loves us within it, offering the grace of daily transformation. The truth sets us free to grow.

Scripture...

You will answer me...

Listen, O Lord, and answer me, for I am afflicted and needy.
Preserve my life for I am God-fearing; save your servant who trusts in you.
Have mercy on me, O Lord, for I cry to you all day.
Bring joy to the soul of your servant, for you, O Lord, I lift up my soul.
You are good and forgiving, O Lord, caring for those who call on you.
Listen, O Lord, to my prayer, hear the voice of my pleading.
I call on you in the time of my trouble for you will answer me.

Psalm 86:1–7

We pray...

God of truth

and justice,

shed your light

on the dark places

of our lives.

Help us to see ourselves

with your eyes,

truthful but compassionate.

May we know ourselves

as loved

and forgiven sinners,

experiencing with gratitude

your love,

new every morning.

Blessed are those
who find
their strength
in you,
whose hearts
are set
on pilgrimage.

Psalm 84:5

unexpected

A prophet on a lonely journey –
the goal: encounter with God.
How do we come
face to face with God?
How will we find
strength for the pilgrimage?
How will we know
that we have found the one we seek?
Our way
is not mapped out in certainties.

We walk by faith and not by sight,
making the path by walking.
So many choices to discern.
Life shakes the sure ground
under our feet.
The wind of change
strips away our protective covering.
The fire of our passions
blazes all around us.

In the midst of the chaos,
the sound of a gentle breeze.
God enters our life quietly,
like April dew on the grass,
like a drop of water on a sponge,
like a leaf falling into the palm
of an open hand.

unexpected

Elijah lived in a shifting world, threatened by abusive power and a culture of death. Isolated in his commitment to truth, he felt like the last remnant of the faithful, surrounded by the voices of unbelief. God challenged his doubt and despair: 'Can you trust me to sustain you on your journey? Can you be open to meeting the God of surprises?' The unremarkable, unobtrusive God who speaks in whispers meets him in the cave in a way that stretches the limits of his imagination. Open to the unexpected, Elijah receives power to become a prophetic presence in a hostile world.

Scripture...

God of surprises

Glory to God who shows his power in us and can do much more
than we could ask or imagine; glory to him in the Church
and in Christ Jesus through all generations for ever and ever. Amen

Ephesians 3:20–21

We wait for a new heaven and a new earth in which justice reigns,
according to God's promise. Therefore, beloved, as you wait in expectation of this,
strive that God may find you rooted in peace, without blemish or fault.

2 Peter 3:13–14

We pray...

God of surprises,

God of the unexpected,

you approach us delicately,

whispering your presence

amid the noise

of our world.

Make us sensitive

to the sound of your name

echoing

in the quiet places

where you wait for us.

They called
to the L*ORD*
in their trouble
and he rescued them
from their sufferings,
reducing the storm
to a whisper
until the waves
grew quiet.

Psalm 107:28–29

be calm

Life at its most chaotic,
pressure at its worst.
The boat of our life adrift
on raging seas,
tossing us up and down
in terrifying storms.

But our efforts to save ourselves
come to grief.
No rudder to guide us,
oars breaking
as we pull against the tide.
We can't bail ourselves out.

Sinking beneath the waves of crisis,
we feel outraged.
'Where are you, God,
when we feel shipwrecked?
Don't you care that we are sinking?
Why won't you wake up
and do something?'

A voice of power
speaks above the storm:
'I made the sea and the sky.
I ride on the wings of the storm.
Why are you afraid?
Peace!
Be still, and know that I am God.'

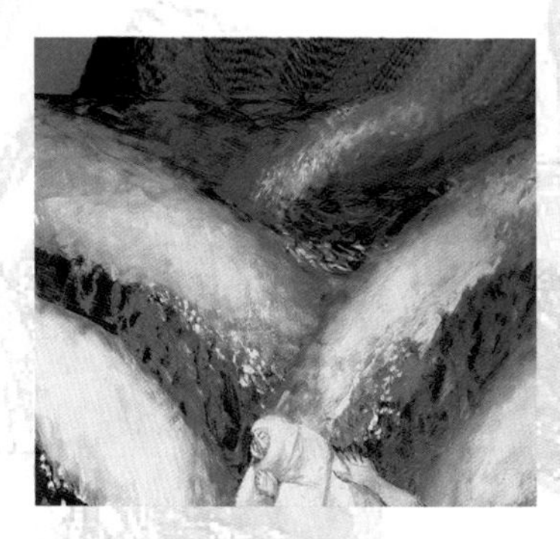

be calm

Our daily life can feel rock-solid and predictable. We think we control so much – even the weather. In the quiet havens of life being close to God is easy, secure in the love and care of a compassionate and reassuring presence. But life's storms can hit us unawares, tossing us into a sea of uncertainty, cutting us off from all that feels safe. This is when we are challenged to move from faith as notional assent to lived reality. God doesn't play deliberately hard to get, but invites us to learn true dependence through knowing our fragility. Blessed are we when we know our need of God.

Scripture...

Do not fear

God is our strength and protection, an ever-present help in affliction.
We will not fear, therefore, though the earth be shaken
and the mountains plunge into the seas,
though its waters foam and roar, though the mountains quake and totter.
For the Lord of hosts is with us, the God of Jacob, our stronghold.
Be still and know that I am God.

Psalm 46:1–3,7,10

We pray...

God of stillness and storm,

you are greater

than our plans and designs,

more powerful

than our attempts

to be in control.

Guide us

through life's uncertainties.

Calm us in times of tempest.

Shake us in our complacency.

Teach us to know

that you alone are God.

In God's hand
is the soul
of every living thing
and the breath
of every human being.

Job 12:10

stronghold

How good it feels to be sure of myself!
How gratifying to feel
the admiring gaze of others.

Weaknesses can be glossed over,
it's better to rely on my strengths.

Substance isn't too important,
it's all a matter of presentation…

How risky to step into the unknown –
safer to stay behind,
letting others dare who will.
No fear of failure that way!

An invitation comes to
take a step forward,
but not in the strength of our own ego.

God's weakness, our strength,
God's gamble, our certainty.

Do we dare to reach out
and grasp that wounded hand?

stronghold

Football slogans proclaim that today's sporting personalities walk on water. It is an expression for someone who is trusted to pull off miracles and deliver a star performance. That's easier said than done. We are caught in a dilemma: risk is frightening and dangerous, and may lead to humiliating failure, but fear and insecurity prevent growth and keep us stunted. God longs for us to reach out in faith, in order to give us the courage we need to grow into our truest self. Simon, the fisherman, had to learn to sink before becoming Peter the Rock.

Scripture...

The hand of the Lord

For I am the Lord, your God,
who grasps your right hand:
it is I who say to you:
Do not fear,
I will help you.

Isaiah 41:13

We pray...

God of uncertainty,

you call to us

across the storm.

We long to come to you

but fear to step

on unsure ground.

Help us to trust

that your strong hand

holds us

in our weakness.

I have just given you
an example
that as I have done,
you also may do.

John 13:15

washing of feet

Feet and hands:
work-worn hands
reach out in love.
Indecisive hands respond,
embracing and repulsing.

Our hands held out to God:
'Come close, but not too close,
touch me, but don't ask me to change!'

Washing of feet –
the work of a wife or a slave.
Too menial,
too intimate a gesture for the Master.

'If you want to be my companion,
let me touch you,
prepare to be changed,
have the courage to be like me.'

Bread broken, a body broken,
a cup poured out for us.

An example of humblest service:
'Do you see what I have done?
Do this in my memory.'

washing of feet

By washing the disciples' feet Jesus shows us the trademark of those who follow him – humble service. The Eucharist cannot be separated from this gesture of love and humility. It is at once the most sacred sign and the most human. We only re-enact it once a year in our liturgy, but it is re-enacted every day in our simple acts of kindness. Peter's response to Jesus serves as a warning to us. Being a giver can put us in a position of superiority. We are not the Messiah! Can we let ourselves be served as well as serve? Can we let Christ touch us through the hands and service of others?

Scripture...

Lord and Master

When Jesus had finished washing their feet,
he put on his garment again,
went back to the table and said to them,
'Do you understand what I have done to you?
You call me Master and Lord, and you are right, for so I am.
If I, then, your Lord and Master, have washed your feet,
you also must wash one another's feet.
I have just given you an example that as I have done, you also may do.'

John 13:12–15

We pray...

Lord Jesus,

Servant King,

you set aside your glory

to become our slave.

You touch us

in intimate love.

Help us to know you

in our service of others,

in theirs to us,

in the breaking of bread

and the washing of feet.

Then they told their story
of what had happened on the road
and how they had recognised him
at the breaking of bread.

Luke 24:35

last supper

The face of Jesus
reflected in many places:
a cup of wine at a meal among friends,
living water in the depths of a well,
a towel used to wipe
the face of a condemned criminal,
a bowl of water, washing feet.

What is the meaning of this
breaking of bread,
this new covenant in flesh and blood?

Christ present in so many ways,
blest and broken,
offered and shared.

Whenever we gather together,
when we serve and are served,
when we touch another's suffering,
we are one with God
and each other.
Communion.

God with us
in the features of a thousand faces,
in the simplest of human gestures,
in the sharing of a meal.

The sacred and the simple –
all signs of God's presence.

last supper

Word and sacrament, service and companionship – these are the signs of Christ's living presence. But the signs are not confined to the sanctuary, kept safe and sacred in a holy place. These signs are offered to us every day in the simplicity of human experience, as Jesus taught us. 'But when did we see you hungry or thirsty, sick or in prison, naked or lonely?' 'When you did it to the least of my sisters or brothers, you did it to me.' It is human life itself which offers signs of God's indwelling, if only we have eyes to see.

Scripture...

Take and eat, take and drink

While they were eating, Jesus took bread, said a blessing
and broke it, and gave it to his disciples saying,
'Take and eat; this is my body.'
Then he took a cup and gave thanks, and passed it to them saying, 'Drink
this, all of you, for this is my blood,
the blood of the Covenant, which is poured out for many
for the forgiveness of sins.'

Matthew 26:26–28

We pray...

Risen Lord,

you come to meet us

in so many ways,

hidden

but always present

in our human encounters.

Give us eyes

to see you

and hearts

to recognise you

among the signs you give.

I will give you
the treasures
of darkness
and riches hidden
in secret places.

Isaiah 45:3

understanding

A long and lonely road,
faith shattered,
hearts broken,
'Our hope had been...'
– a world of disappointment
in those words.

A stranger unrecognised
draws out the story,
this is not the God they are used to,
not the outcome they expected.

The Scriptures are opened,
meaning peeled back,
layer after layer.
Truth emerges,
a glimmer of light.
'Stay with us, for darkness is falling.'

God-with-us comes to the table,
breaks bread,
smiles a moment,
and is gone!

'We have seen him,
we have touched him,
he walked beside us,
though unknown!'

What are the signs
of his presence among us,
wounded and risen,
hidden yet revealed?

Hearts burning, minds opened,
faith, hope and love
dawning in the darkness.

understanding

The road to Emmaus is a lesson in discernment. Jesus does not give a lecture in theology, but opens up a circle of meaning. Reflecting on the Scriptures, the deep significance of lived reality is understood. Reading Scripture in the light of lived reality, the word of God becomes clear. Each is needed if life is to make sense in the light of faith. The invitation is to detect signs of the resurrection in the small events of daily life, the hidden God waiting to be revealed.

Scripture...

Signs of the resurrection

We prove we are true ministers of God in every way by our endurance in so many trials, in hardships, afflictions, floggings, imprisonment, riots, fatigue, sleepless nights and days of hunger.
People can notice in our upright life, knowledge, patience and kindness, action of the Holy Spirit, sincere love, words of truth and power of God.
So we fight with the weapons of justice, to attack as well as to defend.
Sometimes we are honoured, at other times insulted; we receive criticism as well as praise. We are regarded as liars although we speak the truth; as unknown though we are well known; as dead and yet we live. Punishments come upon us but we have not, as yet, been put to death. We appear to be afflicted, yet always joyful; we seem to be poor, but we enrich many; we have nothing, but we possess everything!

cf 2 Corinthians 6:4–10

We pray...

Lord of Calvary and Easter,

God of surprises.

When sorrow and doubt

overwhelm us,

give us eyes of faith

to see you in the Scriptures,

in the breaking of bread,

in your everyday glory.

the artist

Sieger Köder was born on 3rd January 1925 in Wasseralfingen, Germany, where he also completed his high school studies. During the Second World War, Sieger Köder was sent to France as a front line soldier; there he was made a prisoner of war in 1944-45. Once freed, Köder studied engraving and silversmithing. He attended the Academy School of Art in Stuttgart until 1951 and then studied English philology at the University of Tübingen as part of his qualification as a teacher.

After 12 years of teaching art and working as an artist, Köder undertook theological studies for the priesthood, and in 1971 he was ordained a Catholic priest. From 1975 to 1995, Fr Köder was parish priest in Hohenberg and in Rosenberg. He then retired in Ellwangen, not far from Stuttgart, where he now lives.

The years of Köder's parish ministry are among the most prolific with inspiring works of art. There is complete synergy between Fr Köder being a minister and an artist. He uses his paintings as Jesus used his parables. He reveals the depth of the Christian message through metaphors and by shedding light and colour on human history. Thus we understand why Köder's art is heavily charged with the experience of the Nazi period and the time of the Holocaust.

Köder's paintings are also rich with theological insight. He shows a certain reserve in representing the figure of Jesus, who most of the time is outside the scene – in the position of the viewer – to convey the idea that Jesus is alive today in the person of the viewer. Köder dips his brush into the very essence of the Gospel and with colour describes the wholeness of human life. Thus, his art is a vibrant glimpse of the depth, the length and the width of the mystery of Christ in each one of us.

The images of Sieger Köder's paintings are also available as posters, digital images, postcards and prayer cards. For complete information please visit our website at ***www.pauline-uk.org***.

the author

Gemma Simmonds is a sister of the Congregation of Jesus. She lectures in pastoral theology and spirituality at Heythrop College, University of London and has a background in teaching, university and prison chaplaincy and spiritual direction. She has a wealth of experience using the paintings of Sieger Köder in lectures and retreats in many different countries, and she continues to find something new in the images every time she uses them.

Writing with a reflective and perceptive gaze, Gemma has shared depth and richness of insight into Köder's work. She sees symbols and themes in the images that link to Scriptures and opens up a meaningful reflective space for others to consider and be enriched by these powerful images.

Gemma is author of ***Glimpses of the Divine,*** another title in the series on ***The Art and Inspiration of Sieger Köder*** published by Pauline Books & Media.

The Closeness of God *is one of the many resources produced by the Daughters of St Paul, an international Catholic community of religious women dedicated to spreading the Good News of Jesus Christ. In imitation of the Apostle Paul, who used every means to proclaim Christ, the sisters work with modern media and technology for evangelisation.*

There are four Pauline Books & Media Centres in the UK and an on-line catalogue (www.pauline-uk.org) of Pauline resources produced by us: a wide variety of excellent materials that are Scripture-based, attractive and practical.